The Voice of God

Christian Poems

NIGEL S. DARING

The Voice of
God

Christian Poems

NIGEL S. DARING

ARPress

ARPress
45 Dan Road Suite 15
Canton MA 02021
Hotline: 1(888) 821-0229
Fax: 1(508) 545-7580

Ordering Information:
Quantity sales. Special discounts are available on quantity purchases by corporations, associations, and others. For details, contact the publisher at the address above.

Printed in the United States of America.

ISBN-13:   Softcover   979-8-89676-183-9
              eBook   979-8-89676-184-6

Library of Congress Control Number: 2025913070

TABLE OF CONTENTS

Come unto me, all ye that labor and are heavy laden, and I will give you rest –
Matthew 11 verse 28

Acknowledgements

A work like this can only be done under the guidance and inspiration of the living God. Therefore, I first give thanks to God Almighty for all His blessings bestowed, especially with regards to this project. I am eternally grateful to my Father in Heaven who renders His wisdom and understanding. I declare that the words written in this book are more than mine. They are His funneled through me.

I am also grateful to human components who God put in my way. I mention Vivia Brown in particular who has been constantly supportive in my life. She has always thought the best of me and has never failed to encourage me at my worst. With her kindness and care, I am always reminded that there are beautiful people in the world to whom I owe much gratitude.

I thank other individuals who have not only been fans of my work, but who have also been supportive, even to the extent of doing a lot of leg work to advertise and promote what I've done. I appreciate Rita Kane who expended such energy on my behalf without my even asking it of her. I thank Andrea Catalina Monroy who has decided of her own accord to translate one of my books in Spanish. I also want to thank Paris Dennis who has not ceased speak about my works and my person to friends and family. I certainly look forward to working with him in the future on a number of projects.

Throughout the years I've developed a fan base. Names are too plentiful to list. But I really want to send my love to all of them. I produce here another work that should strengthen their respect for my talent, but more so a work that they should find satisfying to their spiritual welfare.

Again, thanks one and all. God bless.

Introduction

The professed Christian will love reading this book. It contains one hundred poems that appeal to his or her sense of values. Many works herein can be used as devotionals. Much of the poems may be regarded as messages of encouragement and enlightenment. The entire body of work supports a positive look at self and the world through the gospel of Jesus Christ. The book supports mission on Christ's behalf and salvation through His love. It reminds the reader of the power of faith and prayer. It calls him or her to duty inspired by the love Jesus displayed. The book also relays Christ's hope of eternal reward for those guided by His faith and baptized in His blood.

Today the world drifts ever so insidiously towards moral decay, instability, and fear. Now more than ever Jesus' message is needed to recalibrate mankind's thinking and approach. If people can realize the great values He articulated, internalize them, and try to spread them, the status of the world would be much better. This book proudly contributes to that effort. It is an honest contemplation of the Bible through poetry, particularly focusing on Jesus' message of salvation for mankind.

One can use these poems to reflect on Jesus' life, example, and teachings. He or she can find important facets of these captured in beautiful phrases and poems. They reinvigorate spirit, captivate mind, and motivate par action. The reader is reminded that God should take priority in his or her life and have that value condition his or her deeds. The book argues that this is the essence of Jesus Christ and what He meant for mankind. This final line in the first stanza of the first poem "Praise with Pleasure" captures the idea: "Lord you're all that's right for me to do".

Make no mistake, by following the advice and learning from the morals contained in this book, one will certainly improve himself personally, emotionally, and spiritually. This is a book that promotes time-honored values through which people of all kinds have found balance in their lives, inspiration, and fulfillment. One can read it daily and find great reward from doing so.

PRAISE WITH PLEASURE

Lord your Word is the fire in my soul
Your Spirit courses as streams through my veins
There's no life for me without you
You're the sight I see through
Lord you're all that's right for me to do

You've been with me in my lonely days
You carried my burdens when I needed help
You were sincere when you dried my tears
Lord, you've never failed me through the years
You're all that's right in my life

I praise you with unreserved pleasure
I devote all I can claim to you
I only aim for you
My soul aches for you
You're my only satisfaction

Glory be to the heavens that hold you
Blessed be all your handiwork
Wondrous is its cherished beauty
Miraculous appears the design of it all
Creation declares your magnificent splendor

Comforted are they showered by your grace
Enlightened are they who grasp your wisdom
Strengthened are they richened by your Spirit
Emboldened are they in the power of your might
Uplifted are they whose hearts you've touched

The faithful treasure your tender mercies
Oh Lord, how could I forget?
Your kindness restored me
Your grace reassured me
I stand tall because on your name I did call

I dedicate myself wholeheartedly for what you've done
There's nothing comparable to what you mean to me
No one takes priority over you
For you, I make myself available
Unto you I give all that I'm able

Every breath I take is for you,
For I know each breath is of you
You put me on Earth for a purpose
I live for nothing but its fulfillment
May you find my life fruitful in your sight

I will worship you Lord with heart, mind, and tongue
I'll teach as many as are willing to do the same
Regard me as an angel in your Kingdom,
For the glory of your way is my light
Serving you is all there is to my life

HELP THE NEEDY

I'd like to help all in need but I can't
So I ask Lord, help all those in want
Forsake them not in their trials
And show me whoever I can help with whatever I have

There are too many who live unspeakable sorrow
Misery and insufficiency have left their lives hollow
Their situation doesn't have to be hopeless
Lord, I beg you to improve their condition
Let them live properly as humans

Use me Lord, use me to make a difference
For this cause I give you deference
And let me use you as reference
When I testify with all reverence
How by your aid I was able to aid
And made many no longer afraid

My position isn't the best but it's not the worst
There're many who're worse,
As if their life is a curse
Please make them blessed
And let me do my very best
Let them pass if their situation is a test
You can help, as I can attest,
To elevate them from some wretched problem

Lord this is a heartless and cold world we live in,
All because of sin
Many just care for themselves and no one else,
Chasing inexorably after personal wealth
Others suffer inexcusably due to their greed
Their prosperity leaves many in need

But Father I only see success as equal progress,
So I want to convince those with more to help those with less
And I want to be an example of this philosophy I possess
Lord help me with this process

BIBLE IN MY BRAIN

Looking through the Bible plastered on my face I saw beauty in life and
redemption for mankind
Then said I to myself, "It's better buried in my mind"
So infectious was it, it spread through my brain,
Becoming its very neurons while releasing my pain

My words were of the good book,
As well as my thoughts and outlook
It made me conscious
And my deeds righteous

Every time I read I see something new
Even the very same verse will give a different view,
Depending on where I'm at in life
And how I now view the strife

The words of the Bible are immeasurably beautiful
Its power to comfort is beyond wonderful
Oh how sweet it is to have it in me
It's God Himself within my mind setting me free

So much of it is a code
When I read it with a pure mind, I can decode
And whilst in my mind it rests,
Temptations in me it arrests

The words of the Bible are the Word
I claim myself sheep and it shepherd
I've surrendered my very will
To the Word residing in me still

Reading the Bible lifts the words as vapor,
Which soaks in my mind as they are on paper
The more I read the more I act by its prod,
Behaving righteously as I possess the mind of God

UNCONDITIONAL LOVE

Where I was born matters not
It's where I end that counts
Only fools value my color
God only cares for my character

The sun that shines on you shines on me
We were all born equal and free,
Until society distinguished
But in my mind such notions I've extinguished

If you have a good heart, you're my brother
We may or may not fellowship together
But in the Spirit of the Lord, we are one
Where good souls are, there we will be

My love of God makes me love others,
Regardless of their background or culture
The Spirit of the Lord conditions me to help all in need,
Not just a select few who share my identity

I feel all people in me as I feel the Lord within
Human suffering anywhere aggrieves me
Mankind's welfare is my deepest care
The Spirit of the Lord brings me there

Innocent babies deserve a world of love
They're more than human offspring;
They're God's children
Loving them unconditionally is all our responsibility

Our primary purpose is to live to God's pleasure
It's my sole goal, my soul goal
Loving each other without prejudice makes God happy
I won't subject myself therefore to hating others unfairly

I want the Lord to remember me for living a full life,
A life full of love for all His creatures,
A life dedicated to humanity's better,
A life that brought Him great pleasure

RESET MY LIFE

Lord calm my unsteady nerves
Steady my trembling heart
Ease my troubled mind
Comfort my disturbed soul

Today shows me anguish
The morrow brings sorrow
Burden floods the future
Hope avoids my vision

A rain of tears sieges my banks within
The pain of years besieges my thanks thin
My fears have overwhelmed my confidence
Agony wears my constituent with fury beyond intense

Lord take revenge on my hurt
Resurge life within my spirit
Get me the balance I need
Reset me this instance I plead

Impossible in my eyes is possible in yours
My hope fully rests with you Lord
My confidence builds reflecting on you
My constitution is calm reflecting you

Lord justify my great faith
Give me evidence to cling on
Alleviate my distressed situation
With all there is in me I trust you

Others have testified of your mercy
Their love brought them blessings
My love of you is ever as true
I expect no lessening

PRAYERS

My prayer left my mouth as tufts of wind,
But arrived unto the Lord as a weight
Heavy in His hand He considered it
He uttered His Word,
Which was unto Him light as wind,
But reached me as a weight,
Impacting my life with the moment of change

Even when my prayers seep out my thoughts,
The Lord gathers them as a weight,
Never casts He them in the bin of history
Seriously He handles them;
Powerfully felt are His answers
I have prayed formally and leisurely:
In meditation with scripture;
While I stroll in the grassy park

I have prayed in the morning, noontime, and evening,
Before I sleep and in the middle night

I have prayed by myself and in company

I have prayed concerning mighty matters
And the least of concerns

The Lord treasures all my prayers
They bring Him pleasure
And in pleasure He gives each its due

Oftentimes I pray and imagine an answer
How foolish is my imagination to set expectation
I'll only be disappointed and lose faith
It's better to wait,
And let my expectation be of the Lord
Then I'll realize,
He answered my prayer better than I ever imagined

WHAT'S IMPORTANT

My shape doesn't shapen or sharpen my mind
My body isn't as important as my body of work
My height is only as good as my height of wisdom
My weight is as heavy as the weight of truth I possess
My word is empty unless I express the Word
My eyes are useless if I see not the Light of the World
My walk is misdirected unless it's in the way of the Lord
My heartbeat only matters if it beats to the rhythm of love

If what I find can't bring me peace of mind, then what good is it?
If I've gotten my gains by dishonesty, should I count myself honorable
for the possession of them?
Will I ever be accomplished if I've never fulfilled my purpose?
Does it profit me to gain the world and lose my soul?

The man rich in spirit possesses wealth indeed
A man can't savor his wealth if in gaining he sacrificed his health
The fool with money shall end in penury
Possession is useless to he whose wants can't be satisfied
He who lacks appreciation of what he has can't appreciate what he
desires
The lover of money and materials can't be satisfied by money and
materials
The man that has but lacks humanity has nothing to boast about
He with much material wealth draws much company but never true
love

As I ponder such matters, I consider what it is that really matters:
Oh my soul, oh my soul,
The Lord God
What should be exalted above and beyond God?
There's nothing conceivable
For all gained, He can take away
All that's needed He can give

What love greater than His can I find?
What other wisdom is there for my mind?
Then say I to myself,
"Soul be content and love the Lord"

THE VOICE OF GOD

As rolling thunder and oceans of water is the voice of God
But meek is it in the mind of man
From the humble baa of a lamb to the roar of a lion,
His Truth spans creation
The throne of Zion echoes through a carpenter,
Healing the sick by faith,
Giving salvation to hearts frayed
Joyous at the answering are souls who've prayed
The Lord God prized and apprized their voice

In a simple manger is Christ born,
The cry of a babe with a voice to transform
The little captured for a testament is sufficient;
It'll divide history as mankind values it
Through time, it'll give compass to the lost in spirit
It'll comfort the yearning, sweeping their imagination with hope
And provide righteousness in its very scope

Mary, blessed are you to have this child to hold
Blessed are they to have the man to behold
Blessed are the generations who hold Him in their heart
Blessed are they fortified by His ramparts
Blessed are those who have His voice inspire their thoughts
Wise are they led forthwith by His words
Their victory is assured by His might and right

In the wilderness, the voice of a wild man prophesies
Above the chosen one, the voice of God affirms
On Him God by a dove does pitch, resonating through His pitch
From the river Jordan across oceans the voice reverberates,
Offering redemption to all who'd cheerfully receive
And the promise of Heaven to all who believe
They raise His voice, the Gospel of His saving grace,
Spreading a divine message across the human race,
Giving optimism for a prism to a world in need of vision

THE STORM

An anguished man pours out his soul to Heaven
In the downpour upon a grassy plain the pitter patter of rain hit him vehemently with awakening in beats
Upbeat as lightning strikes before him, his mind lightens up with clarity never known prior,
Priority shifting as thunder rolls from Heaven through his belly
He rises from his knees as Christ rising from the tomb,
Zestful with the chest full of damp air he's inhaling,
Hailing the certitude grafting his attitude
His life has been repurposed with a focus illuminated by divine grace
His mind trained upon his goal, he strides somberly pondering,
Wondering at his blessing by the touch of God through the storm
For his life was in a storm and in a storm was it washed away
And through the storm he found life, another way,
A vision beyond the dark cloud,
And verve to unshroud a new day
Praises be to the Lord, the God of creation who moves creation to help the faithful

WALKING

Walking barefooted on dirt,
I feel the current of the Earth,
Rushing through me on contact,
Settling in my system,
Establishing rhythm with nature

Walking in the Spirit,
I feel the power of Heaven,
Bombarding me with grace,
Comforting my soul,
Uniting me with the Lord

Walking amongst people,
I feel their energy,
Touching my being with concern,
Making my heart pump love,
Circulating my all with brotherhood

Walking with the animals,
I feel their vibrance,
Embracing my core,
Enticing me for more,
Making me sense I'm animal too

Walking through the trees,
I feel their breeze,
Putting me at ease,
Feeding off their life,
Eating from the Tree of Life

Walking by the waters,
I feel their flow,
Reaching within in tides of overflow,
Drinking from the wellspring of life,
Quenching thirst from the life of Christ

COMPASSION FOR THE LORD

Lord I ask you for compassion
But I have compassion on you
You created paradise for us,
But all we've done is harm it
Sickening it must be for you to see

Lord you made us perfect,
Reflections of your being
But we've followed the Devil,
Thinking ourselves incomplete
In shame we change ourselves,
Pursuing false identities,
Reshaping our mentalities,
As well as our bodies
Heart-wrenching for you to watch

Lord you're the perfect Father
You care for us all
Yet we don't care for you at all
You teach us good values,
Which most of us ignore
Terrible for you to face this

Lord I know you punish,
But it gives you no pleasure
We're your children;
Damning us for sin hurts you
I feel bad you must bear this

I'll do my best to increase your joy at us
I'll spread your good Word,
Let people know you love them
And to abandon sin
I feel bad for you
But I want you to feel good at what I do

GOD SOLVES ALL

On concrete he sleeps,
Watching feet like heartbeat
Silently he weeps,
Hope wandered in the heat

She passes by,
Drops him a dime
In her soul is a cry,
Profession like crime

She reports to a boss,
Awaiting her report
He can't stand a loss
For vanity they export

He has a family,
Which he hardly sees
Bawls his little girl Emily,
Lonely drowns her in seas

Souls in need of salvation,
They have different issues,
But have the same solution
None need her or his shoes

God is there with comfort
And He inspires the best
There's no need to hurt,
He gives peace and rest

Hope, love for the forsaken,
Morality for those with duty,
Satisfaction for souls shaken,
The Lord gives life its beauty

WARRIORS OF TRUTH

Joshua shouted to the sun to stand still,
Battle not yet done
Keep shining light of the world,
Till the army of God triumphs

The Lord sent His only begotten Son
The faithful shout unto Him mightily
He stays the Light of the World undimmed,
Warriors of Truth illuminated whilst fighting evil

Israel marched around Jericho seven days,
Blowing trumpets inspiring the troops
Seven angels will blow trumpets in Zion,
Rallying warriors of Truth fighting Babylon

Jericho did fall as will Mystery Babylon
The future will be as it was in history
Men haven't learned their lesson
As taught by the Biblical story

By God's word Abraham readied his son for sacrifice,
But caught himself a lamb instead as God commanded
The Lord sacrificed His Son as a lamb to the slaughter,
Victory for the warriors of Truth in His resurrection

God wrote Truth upon Moses' tablets of stone
Jesus wrote wisdom upon ground for one not to be stoned
He inscribed it in the conscience,
Guide for warriors of Truth battling hypocrisy

By an ass was Truth spoken
Upon an ass Truth had ridden
As the ass saved the prophet,
So did the prophet save believers
(And led the warriors of Truth as King)

FULFILLING DIVINE PURPOSE

From the womb of our biological mother to the womb of mother Earth
we go
In between we have a chance to have meaning
It's only a brief opportunity to do something
What we have to offer is in our nature
We need to execute the plan God determined
We must know ourselves to know what we possess,
Seeking God's blessings to explore and expose it in the process
Victory is innate to our being
Failure is neglect of our nature

In faith we were conceived
Through faith we must conceive
By faith we must believe
With faith we will receive

God planned to back us at conception,
So let's have Him in our conception
He'll provide all the resources we need,
If we resource ourselves to His deed

Friends and family are often barriers
Sometimes they're backbiters and news carriers
But we shouldn't live for them
We can't let their folly be our problem

Many times, the world puts up obstacles
Mission seems impossible through our spectacles
But in time we'll overcome,
If we never give up and apply wisdom

Years we may be drowning in tears
Years we may be down in fears
Many times, it seems better in an average career
But wisdom says that'll never take us there

Persistence and insistence are key,
As well as hanging on to the Almighty
One man determined can change the world
By having God's Truth sealed within unfurled

We each have that power
We all can tower
God is our very essence
Let our life be about revealing His presence

RIGHTEOUS THOUGHTS

When you curse a righteous man, you curse God
To disrespect anyone unfairly is an offense to God
If you provoke a man to wrath when you could've stirred a peaceful
answer, you likewise stir God's anger
Where you treat a human inhumanely, God will multiply in your life
the pain you've caused

A just man's reward is the blessing of God
He who walks in the beauty of His holiness shall reside in paradise
A righteous heart produces fruits of God's glory
He rich in God's spirit represents God on Earth

The wise man seeks to become a richer person spiritually
The fool despises God's instruction
He sets himself up for destruction
But the wise uses morality for construction

The optimist sees beauty in the morning rise
He counts whatever he has with joy
The wretched in spirit focuses on what he lacks
Greed infatuates him to a tormenting

The honor of the ungodly is bestowed upon the ungodly
But righteous people refrain from such praise
And seek for themselves the honor of angels
Fools seek fame to the disdain of their souls

Those living in spirit can discern evil spirits in flesh
Wiser is he who seeks comfort within than he who searches the world
for satisfaction
Humility is the stead of the confident
Arrogance leads fools to shame

NO GREATER LOVE

For the love of man you were willing to be killed
For the love of God you were being killed
For the love of man you forgave your killers,
Even while you were being killed
How great a love you possess
So great a love you possess
That you could look at your killers and forgive
And because you did,
Man found courage to live
And you found spirit to rise from the tomb,
In rebirth as a child from his mother's womb

Man found salvation in your resurrection
Man could be reborn in spirit as you were in flesh:
Man could be reborn in spirit by your rebirth in flesh
Through your great love for man,
Man found the love of God
In your example, man found principle:
Forgive and live,
And give your life for humanity
Herein lies true morality

While freeing man from the chains of sin,
You laid on him a burden
Your love displayed outweighed any known
Man's love must be measured by what was shown
Through your love, man envisions Heaven
By its saving grace, man can unite the human race

Man spared not your life
But you spared theirs
And in your life man found eternal life
By your love man knew paradise,
And rebirth in spirit,
The spirit that resurrected you

POWER OF PRAYER

When all hope was fading,
We lived in dreaded fear
Desire burned in our chest
We needed breakthrough
We had given it our best,
But all fell through
We would've given more,
Only the spirit was willing,
But the flesh was weak
We only had prayer

In prayer we found confidence
It became our hope,
Our rock to cling on in unsteady waters,
Wall to pin our dreams on
We were strangely energized by it,
As if it fed our spirit,
And put life in our limbs

We don't remember dark days with pleasure
But we remember prayer,
Our light in the dark,
How it gave us a spark
We remember prayer,
How the Lord gave us favor,
How it changed our behavior

Through prayer we found possibility,
A door open when all seemed closed
But it was enough to walk through
And claim our breakthrough
Through prayer we claimed progress
Today we declare it the root of our success
We testify so you'll give it an honest try
Never be blue when prayer can get you through

REASSURED IN THE LORD

Filling my mind with thoughts of you my view becomes clear
My meditation of Zion strengthens me with the courage of a lion
Blessed am I of your reassurance
Lord you're my insurance
I am sheltered in your love,
Perfected in your praise
I am secure when you're my driver,
Even when the way seems unsure,
And it is filled with danger
Lord I'm contended boarding the plane,
If you're the pilot
I'll fly with confidence through any turbulence
I am happy taking the trip,
If you're captain of my ship
I'll certainly keep calm through any storm

The past is the past and what's done is done
The future is yet to come
But why worry what will be,
When you'll be there for me?
I'll savor the present,
Taking comfort in your presence

The faith within me conquers any fear the world presents
Who or what can be greater than you dear God?
Worry is foolish when I've got you
Worry is for the faithless
I'm blessed

DREAM

There's a dream of the yearning soul
It's the dream of the yearning world,
Dream of Heaven to cover the land,
Dream of love the language spoken
May the dream be man's ambition;
May it be the Lord God's intention

Reality is only a dream
By dream we can shape reality
Courage with a dream makes it real
The weak-hearted live by what they see,
Which is what is,
Never what could be

Life is a dream;
When we die, we're waking
Should we wake to the nightmare of our fear?
Or should we wake in the hope that is Heaven?

To lead with conviction is to be led by a dream
Inaction is dream deterred
A weakling has dream deferred
Dream delayed is never to be displayed
The quest of a dream gives life its meaning
Work each day towards a dream, sleep blissful nights in dreams
The righteous man sees his dream as divine purpose
Every soul's fulfillment is a dream realized
A man without a dream lacks principle
A man isn't a man without a dream

Life is the Lord's dream,
But we've made it a nightmare
We can make it a dream again,
If we possess the Lord's vision,
Fulfilling purpose He instills within

LIFE IS A SHOW

It's never the circumstances
It's who we are
Every man's life is a show,
Of which he's the star
We're all actors in a play
We say what role we play
A strong mind plays a strong character
But the stage intimidates a poor actor
The optimist seizes the opportunity
The pessimist complains even with opportunity
The good heart delivers the best performance for the Lord
The evil man performs for those around him,
Really performing for himself in a state of sin

There's no re-run to the show
It's a one-life performance
Each man must decide what he must display,
Whether it be his best,
Or something less,
Not realizing the show is a test

The host of Heaven is the audience
The award is the Crown of Life
And residence in a mansion of eternal paradise,
Hanging out with angels and Jesus Christ

Damnation is for those who don't recognize the moment,
Playing a role for which they weren't meant
Man says which role he plays,
But the wise plays what the Lord lays
The fool thinks the stage is reality;
The wise knows it's a stage of reality
The fool gets caught in the vanity
The wise sees beyond the stage set,
Realizes what's really there to get

A MAN AND HIMSELF

A man comfortable with himself,
Comfortable being by himself
Enjoys emotional health

A man living in spirit,
Rich with the Spirit of God
Has spiritual wealth

A man who can control his emotions,
Controls his body
Dictates his reality

A man who knows himself,
Knows his purpose
Maintains focus

A man with a vision,
Faith and determination,
Manifests his imagination

A man with confidence,
Strength and common sense
Wins in life

A man with hope,
And ability to cope
Endures trials

A man with self-esteem,
Living his dream
Has happiness

A man with morals,
Exhibiting the highest virtues
Has Truth within

LORD YOU'RE MY HOPE

I get tired of living, but I don't want to die
Seems I just need a little space to cry
Lord I'm ready for Heaven,
Just not ready to give up the ghost
You're the Savior,
Save me from this pain I host

It's not bad news
It's just the everyday blues
I want to escape,
But I can't pick and choose
You're my only hope
I've got nothing else to lose

Once I get one thing settled,
Another has me nettled
The Devil never gets weary
But me, I've got a body
Lord stretch forth your hand;
Take me to the promised land

I've got the sweat of death,
And the fret of regret
I'm chained to a world I reject
Freedom seems like a bet
I'm placing my cards on you
Lord, what are you going to do?

I try to take my ease
But this life is like a disease
I try to cure,
But only symptoms, nothing more
Lord, you know the problem
Heal this life of mine I pray

GOD CHANGES MY LIFE

When my body feels like prison
And I'm serving a life sentence,
I pray for it to be more like glass
And I bright light within

Many times it seems I'm moving,
But I don't know where I'm going
Or I'm standing still
And life is taking me for a ride

When lonely becomes my company
And time my worst enemy,
I feel trapped in a moment drifting in forever
Fear like a current runs through my spine
I'm afraid of my own self
And in the past by my shame,
I became someone I never really knew,
Haunted by a self I couldn't own

When nothing makes me happy
And everything makes me sad,
I can't trust the love of anyone
Travail seems like my inspiration
Wail is my sleep for all I fail
Weep so deep until I'm frail
Emptiness soaks in my bones
I feel I belong with dry bones

The Lord takes me from the doldrums,
Saturates my mind with His wisdom,
Replenishes my soul with His love,
Revives my spirit to life anew

My purview is His view
My very being is His,

As is my daily business
The Lord God is my dad
I awake with enthusiasm to the cock crowing,
Growing with the morning with vibrant birds chirping
I rise in the Lord's strength with a grateful prayer
Of the day I'm feeling like a slayer,
Feeling blessed and wonderfully made
I'm high knowing God is standing by
I fly like an eagle in the heavens
I'm in Heaven

With God in me I fill joy in reality
A situation may be negative,
But I'm always positive,
A radiant glow of light in the dark
The Earth is moving
I'm moving the Earth,
Knowing what life is worth
I deserve credit but more so God

JUDGEMENT COMING

Marvelous appears the signs
Angels with timbrels rejoice
The righteous hear God's voice,
The ungodly ears stoppered by sin,
Their eyes blinded by conceit,
While their hearts burn with vile lusts

Wisdom declares her glory
Understanding marches through history,
Escaping the ungodly,
Hailed by them in ignominy,
Battled by their lunacy,
Capsizing them in final victory

The inevitable finds redemption
The righteous persevere to justification
Heaven arrives undeclared,
Except for signs missed by obsessed sinners
Wisdom belongs to the winners
Woe be unto evil partakers

Angels descend with righteous fury
Heathens recognize their penury
God arrives as witness, judge, and jury,
While cherubims open the Garden of Eden
Singing glory hallelujah, saints march in
Awakened to their misery are fools begging

The heathen feel sorry for their bragging
In Heaven begins history for eternity
For the righteous, this is the journey's end,

Which God did portend
And which is a new beginning,
Being life without end with angels as friends

HONESTY IN LIFE

Your face shouldn't be someone else's mask
Your life shouldn't be another man's part
Your family shouldn't be flesh and blood
Your family should be love

Don't work to cover shame,
Get rid of shame
Don't play games,
Be honest with people

Get to know yourself,
You can be honest with yourself
Be honest with God
And He'll give you help

You'll be dishonest seeking people's approval
Seek God's approval and you'll be moral
You'll make a fool of yourself seeking attention,
Not to mention not being true to yourself

Don't pull yourself out of yourself trying to please someone else
Don't be afraid to set limits and let the world know them
Found your standards upon the conscience God implants
Bound yourself by your principles to have self-control

If you must lie to get a job, it's not for you
What's yours requires you to be true
That's what God meant for you to do
Fulfill that purpose as your life's mission

Be honest with yourself,
You can be honest with everyone else
You're the greatest story ever told
Tell it with your life and be bold

GOD IS IN CONTROL

Each day is the Lord's speech
Each breath is His blessing
Let the day suffice itself,
For the Lord will provide
Be grateful breathing His life
We're all at His mercy,
Living on His time
There's nothing for us to claim,
Except the wisdom of our mind

What will the morrow bring?
Man plans and God wipes out
Let's pray He utters favors
And through faith, He'll bring better
Disappointment to the sinner is heartbreak
He binds his ego to his expectations
But in wisdom the wise expects of God,
Knows a plan shattered means better in the future

Where a man's treasure is,
There his heart is also
Wise is he who invests his treasure with the Lord
His eyes will see interest with measure of great reward
God forgets not those who love Him
Trials and tribulations are just for their molding

Birds of the air search for worms
Cheetahs chase after prey
When it's our turn,
Let's be wise and pray
The Lord provides for others,
Why not us His mirrored creatures?
Faith shifts God's hands
We can will Him through love He understands
But in patience we must respect His timing

PROPHET'S LOT

The one they fight the hardest is the prophet
Despised of men, he'll later be revered by them
What is a prophet's reward?
His life is so hard
He sees what others can't see
But what he sees is reality
His difference makes it a lonely life
This is the lot of men of right
But men of light are meant to guide,
Not find place in anonymity to hide
Truth must be spoken,
God's Word unbroken must be uttered by the chosen
Why not, since otherwise He'd have to choose rocks?
The prophet is the rock of God's foundation,
Refused by men in his times
But the stone the builder refused has become the head cornerstone
The descendants of fools regret on the prophet's bones,
Claiming if it had been them they would've known
Want to bet?
The prophet is there yet…

HOME SWEET HOME

There's a place, a land of the free,
Clear blue skies as far as eyes can see,
Where everyone is just a nice guy
And there's no need to be shy
Home sweet home
For the love of the place I cry

It lies beyond the sky
I will have to die
But this isn't my place,
Far too much war in a rat race
Home sweet home
For the love of the place I cry

Land swell with every angel,
Place of peace far from Hell
Devils and angels here mixed,
More devils make it Hell fixed
Home sweet home
For the love of the place I cry

The place is as a dream,
No night and a pure stream
With God the shining light,
Glorious in every sight
Home sweet home
For the love of the place I cry

Sweet Heaven come on Earth
Bring here a new birth
Why must I die to get there,
When love could be right here?
Home sweet home
For the love of the place I cry

SUFFERING MASSES

Struggling masses,
The world divided in classes
I must admit I don't like it
Lord I know it irks your Spirit
Ghetto youths without opportunity,
Mankind without unity;
So many work so hard,
Still life is a bad card

Lord God please intervene
We need you on the scene
Nations put out an image
To the Truth it's sacrilege
Extreme poverty runs rampant
But politicians' lies are constant
So many people turn to crime,
Just to get nickel and dime

Lord we call upon your name
Leaders have left us in shame
They abuse public trust,
Taking bread, leaving us crust
Democracy is what they tote,
But what've we gotten for our vote?
The masses still suffer
While the rich richen their coffer

Bosses say do more with less,
But the salary is still baseless
Inflation on the rise,
Prices too fat for our eyes,
Crises hit our budget,
Basics we can't get
Lord hear our call
Our back is against the wall

CEASE ADDICTIVE BEHAVIOR

Addiction pulls you out of yourself
Whatever you do uncontrollably, repeatedly harms you
It weakens you spiritually
Balance in life is essential
Self-control is fundamental
Greed is a destructive feature of a tormented soul
Recognizing what you naturally need is wise indeed
Simplicity is key
Simple living makes for a peaceful mind
Thinking you need what you don't leads to unnecessary increase,
Stuff that clutters your life,
And augments your stress
Keep to the bare minimum,
Which brings inner peace to its maximum
Cease all behavior to which you're enslaved
Be brave and withstand the pain of withdrawal
Redefine yourself as free of all things material
Determine your world,
Don't let your world determine you
There's only one addiction you should have,
That's addiction to God
Seek Him continually, immensely, intensely
He'll provide all your needs
In faith there's no worry
But addiction is agony
Whatever you get into excessively will control you
Let God control you
But don't let anything of this world do that to you
There's freedom in being God's slave
But a slave of this world lives in sin,
Finds himself perilously chained to whatever he's in,
While his enslaved soul is tortured
Free yourself with God
Possess a free mind and spirit

CONTRASTING INFLUENCES

Vile, evil people listen to the Devil,
Live after his will,
Willing to harm others for their gain,
Even taking pleasure from their pain

The righteous live after God's will,
Making His will their will,
Their likeness His likeness
These are they who God will bless

Demons inveigle to evil
Like eagle after weevil,
They descend on prey,
Those who don't pray

Righteous minds are primed for God
With faith they prime themselves
And remain in their prime,
Prime examples of beings divine

The Devil looks good to the evil
Most see him as god
He doesn't look that odd
That's because their mind is inclined

God is the Light
God is delight
But the Devil appears as an angel of light,
Drawing to Hell who won't give him a fight

It's best to be wise
The Devil one must despise
Love God foremost,
Join His Heavenly host

SPIRITUALITY OVER RELIGION

It's good to be more spiritual than religious,
Or even spiritual and not pious
God resides in our subconscious
We need to be conscious
And have His Truth guide us
In this way let's be ambitious

Religion has a norm,
Rules by which to conform,
Rituals to perform,
Basically, the keeping of form
But it's God that should inform
And religion should be uniform

Religion should express spirituality
Religion shouldn't suppress reality
To put religion above God is vanity
Religion devoid of God is insanity
Religion without God leads to inhumanity
Despite claims, it's really profanity

Don't get me wrong
This isn't an anti-religious song
Religion can make you strong
It does give identity to belong
But just don't go along
Focus on spirituality lifelong

Religion came out of spiritual men
But then there came the heathen,
Having their facade without their spiritual ken
Some became leaders like farmers to hen,
A misinterpretation they did open,
Misleading instead of having minds sharpen

Wise to go back to the root
And not just listen to leaders toot
Truth isn't what they always hoot
Listen to your conscience shoot
Some leaders you give the boot
To God's root you be offshoot

Let's not be misunderstood
Religion is good,
If it's used as it should
To express spirituality, it could
Some do with it as they would
You don't use it for falsehood

Display your best through religiousness
And do not have it express ungodliness
There's enduring Truth in your deepest recess
Tune in to it for your spiritual progress
When you bind with it in oneness,
You'll find true happiness

I REALLY MISS YOU

Long time don't see
You're in Heaven looking at me
Still sorry you did depart
It ripped out a piece of my heart
I miss you dearly
My pain lingers yearly
I pray we'll meet again
In your place of Heaven

You touched my life remarkably
You changed me indelibly
You're my foundation
I'll never forget your contribution
May the angels treat you well
Laugh in pride with them and tell
How you've assisted my growth,
That I'm a wonderful outgrowth

I miss your encouragement
Out of your way for me you went
You taught me self-respect
And how to be more perfect
You told me to use my potential
Because you believed I'm phenomenal
Words can't explain my gratefulness
I'm doing my best with these I express

I give others the support I've known
I believe they can grow as I've grown
Touched by you with a love so true,
I've gotten a clue and my cue
I must do my best to make others their best,
Possess in me the love you had in your chest
In my life you're the greatest example
By your love, through life I can trample

COMPREHENDING SUCCESS

Measure your success by your happiness
The world may be impressed by your career
You may be regarded everywhere
It won't matter if you're not feeling right inside

The amount in your account may be massive
Your possessions may way exceed the average
Your education could be far beyond college
It doesn't matter if you're unfulfilled inside

Success is being yourself
Success is expressing yourself
Success is emotional health
Success is spiritual wealth

If you know who you are
And are committed to that person,
That's success
That's you being your best

Success is the value of the input, not the outcome
Success is the moral value of an achievement
Success is the quality of time spent
Success is about helping others

Success is feeling content
Success is feeling confident
Success is doing your best
Success is happiness

Live your own life
Fulfill your purpose
Be a moral creature
Be at peace
(That's success)

WANTING BETTER SPIRITUALITY

Father, you know who I am
If I'm not worthy of Zion,
Show me my imperfection

Far be it from me to live sinfully
Lord, I want you to be pleased,
Looking into me

I want a pure soul
Help make me whole
Show me how to take control

I'm ashamed of things I've done,
No one else but me to blame
I'm better but perfection is the aim

Lord sharpen my mind to understand
I just want to be the best I can
And live ready for your Kingdom

I've hurt people
I've been hurt before
I don't want to hurt anymore

Show me the way to Zion's door
Let me not be lost in sin
Open my eyes to evil within

You said we can be perfect like you
Anything less for me is unacceptable
I want your way to be my only way

Without sin my spirit is free,
A pleasure to your sight
Lord help me to that right

LESSON LEARNED

I was too blind to see
It was in front of my face
Foolishly I ignored it
It brought a life of disgrace

The veil of expectation covered my eyes,
More so what I wanted fattened my mind
Something was happening that never did fit
It was something unkind I should've left behind

Well, I learned a lesson,
Living with regret
Might as well move on,
Can't be always upset

Lord it's good to recognize your will
And not be obsessed with your own
If I recognized what you ordained,
I would certainly have known

From here on end, I'm committed
It's you I'm thinking about
If you've set what's not for me,
I'm hastily getting out

The world gives you ideals
You try to live up to them
But then you have the real deal
And you realize they're a problem

I won't live by other people's expectations
I don't want my life to be a falsity
Lord you're all I'm living for,
Accepting your ordinance for reality

I CAN TESTIFY

I've seen the power of God
Faith brought me to it
I was amazed, comforted, justified
No longer do I worry,
My God will provide
By my eyes I testify
The experience got me high
Thank you Lord,
You are truly amazing
Thank you for strengthening my faith
My dreams are coming true
Others will come when due
Lord you reassured me

COMFORT IN THE LORD

When something bad happens,
I don't feel stressed
I think you're up to something
I just don't see it yet

Lord you have my trust
I love you too much to doubt
You love me too much to let me down
I'll be patient and wait for you,
Give blessings a chance to come when due

I live at ease without fear
Lord you are there
Of that I'm wholly confident
But I don't sit around complacent
I just perform feeling assured

The day of my due will come
You'll exalt me for what I've done
You aren't blind,
Neither are you forgetful,
Neither are you detached
My effort will be matched
Your blessings may exceed my effort
Because in you my heart took comfort

I'll be like Job
I'll never curse you,
Regardless of the trials I endure
You're there for sure
You'll bless, even in excess

I'll just keep faith,
Wait,
And keep plugging along

FINDING SELF IN GOD

I found myself in God
No more will I claim I'm all about me
I'm all about God
If it's not to His glory,
I want no part of it
If it's not about His worship,
I'll skip

If a man wants to doubt,
Let him doubt
But I know what I'm about
If a man wants to argue,
Let him argue
I know my God is true

I feel great loving God
I feel fantastic working for God
I feel wonderful with God in me
I feel awesome being part of God
With God, life is worth living
With God, life finds its meaning

I was tortured without God,
Living a life reckless and bad
Once I found Him,
I found who I was
And was overjoyed
My joy ensues
I wish you could wear my shoes

I declare without reservation,
Praises be unto the Lord God,
My Savior and My Redeemer
All praises be unto Him,
The Alpha and the Omega

ANCHOR

I'm swinging my anchor up to Heaven
I'll climb my whole life till I get there
I must escape this world of sin I'm drowning in
I refuse, I refuse to die in sin

The rope holds my hope
I'm determined not to be a victim
I'll climb with all my might
Until I save my precious life

Oh angels up high,
Help rescue me
Pull as I try
I must be free

Oh angels up high,
Your land of righteousness,
I must be there
But don't let me drown down here

I don't want to drown in sin
I want to live in righteousness,
In the land of the blessed,
Where everyone does their best

I'll climb with faith and prayer
They'll let me survive rough tides
I'll have love to keep my heart pumping,
Especially when I'm over swept holding my breath

Lord free me from this world of sin
Tug, pull me up, pull me out
With your help, faith, prayer, and love I'll be saved,
Climbing the rope of hope to eternal life

FOOD ADDICTION

I was hungry and ate
But hunger called out to me again
I yielded and gained weight
Again, my hunger arrived with pain

Then wondered I, "How could my body be calling for what it was only
going to store?"
Puzzled was I for sure
I struggled with the concept of wanting but not needing
Then called I to mind Genesis Chapter 1 verse 29:

> And God said, "Behold, I have given you
> every herb bearing seed, which is upon the
> face of all the earth, and every tree, in the
> which is the fruit of a tree yielding seed;
> to you it shall be for meat."

I realized I was addicted to food
My desires were rude
They mirrored those of seasoned drug addicts craving a fix
I wasn't hungry; I was addicted
To unnatural substances my body had adjusted,
Experiencing withdrawal symptoms whenever I ceased having them
for a while
No doubt this was unnatural lifestyle

Herbs and fruits are what's to eat
They should be my meat
They should be my treat
I've got addiction to defeat

THE FEAR OF THE LORD

Sometimes I think I'm doing right when I'm doing wrong
Lord give me the wisdom to understand
I wash my hands in innocence,
For I had not the sense

It was not they that I offended that bothered me,
Nor was it the offense
But Lord it was the idea that I offended you
For that I found no defense (except innocence)

For once I feared death,
Until wisdom burned out my fear
Then could I live,
For in fear I couldn't savor life

But I fear you dear God
Wisdom is the fear of the Lord
For what could this world do?
Can it not only harm flesh?

You Lord can harm body and soul,
So I appeal to you in measure
Give me wisdom and understanding,
So I won't offend you even a bit

In living your Truth if I offend men, so be it
The Truth is an offense but not a sin
In my life, let Truth reign supreme
And you find me worthy of esteem

NEW TECHNOLOGY

Men are excited about new technology,
Thinking look what the future holds
But unless they worship God Almighty,
They'll fall as in days of old

It's as the Tower of Babel
Men lusted greatly after greatness
They did as they were able
But fell for they were faithless

Foolishly they build without spiritual foundation
While they lower their moral capacity,
Arrogantly they claim themselves a great nation
With the whore Babylon as their great city

The stink of their ways will reach Heaven
New wizardry in gadgetry they'll celebrate
And won't seek to be forgiven
For that, God will seal their fate

Look at how many problems there are
Unconscionable men have ignored them,
Preferring to be a star
But when they rise, they'll face a problem

Immorality and the unstable social order,
The fundamental Truth they ignore
Will surely cross their border
And make their life sore

Wisdom recognizes signs of the times
It calls out to prepare
For what's happening are ungodly crimes
While man's mind is beyond repair

DARKNESS OF SIN

Sin is mind-boggling
When you see its extremes,
It's really disturbing
To the righteous mind,
To have any within,
It's really disturbing

Sin gives a poor past,
Some bad memories
A good man takes lessons
Evil men continue along,
Sinning without regret,
Like God isn't upset

Love brings unity,
But sin destabilizes
It undermines trust,
Promotes evil lusts
It degrades humanity
Because it's insanity

Sin has bad timing
It's never right
It's never welcome
But men bring it
It's neurotic habit
Being sin's slave

Sin doesn't save
It misbehaves
It has no care
You do it in fear
Rid yourself of it
And sin no more

HUMILITY

When have you heard of a king serving his servants?
There's one who washed His servants' feet
And insisted He do it
Or He wanted no part of them

He set the example of humility
It's the Truth God favors as relayed through the Savior:
He who would exalt himself should humble himself
Only so does he belong in God's Kingdom

Jesus did say, "Whoever is great among you let him be your minister"
To exalt oneself is sinister
Those carrying the Gospel of Christ should minister unto the least fortunate,
Seeing themselves as fortunate (to be their servants)
Only so will they be exalted in the Kingdom of Heaven

Humility is the stead of the wise
Fools live in arrogance
But pride goes before destruction,
And a haughty spirit before a fall

Why should men not be humble?
If the Lord God can visit the Earth and wash men's feet,
Why then should men not follow His example?
As His faith and power lie in His humility,
So does our humility reveal our faith and power
As His greatness was in His service to humanity,
So should our glory rest in our service to humanity

Humility is the key to Heaven
Arrogance is the doorway to Hell
Humility reveals spiritual strength
Arrogance is deficit of contentment

TOWARDS A BETTER WORLD

If we all pitch in, the world can be a better place
The world needs you
The world needs me
The world needs everybody

Faith moves mountains
Love calms the sea
Unity bridges lands
Hope brings possibility

We've got to have the vision
And give it adequate determination
Let's join hands across nations
That'll improve our situation

Let's give due respect,
Use the best of our intellect
Let's end the rat race,
Be a part of the human race

Different keys play in harmony,
Making sweet music
Why can't we?
Imagine what life could be

Life could be a lovely song,
Black and White in unison
Love plays the keys,
Melody putting souls at ease

It takes all colors
It takes all cultures
It takes you and me
It takes everybody

TO WEEP, TO WAIL

To weep, to wail
To hope, to fail
Land of the free,
Home of the brave
So welcoming,
Welcomes in
Hireling and slave

To weep, to wail
To hope, to fail
Trail of tears
Trail of fears
Dancing spirit
Free in spirit
Free marching

To weep, to wail
To hope, to fail
Land sits still,
Takes blood spill
Justice rides
Darkness hides
God's sun eyes

To weep, to wail
To hope, to fail
Waters dirtied,
Air polluted
New wind blows
Woken by it throes,
Love freely flows

To weep, to wail
To hope, to fail
Bridges build
Place is filled
Roam dear pain,
Rome built again
Christ returns

To weep, to wail
To hope, to fail
Freedom rides
Rights rise
Word sounds
Hope resounds
Christ beckons

To weep, to wail
To hope, to fail
Protests held
Unfairness spelled
Dance free spirits,
In the spirit of Christ
Utter in Christ's voice

MYSTERIOUS WAYS OF GOD

It wasn't what I asked for,
But it's what I got
Then did I consider it
And realized it was better
The Lord works in mysterious ways
It's best never to curse Him,
But to always keep praying
He does answer prayers
And grants strange favors,
Which upon consideration,
Become strangely familiar

Faith is a bridge to God
By faith man gets blessing
Angels walk from Heaven to Earth,
Like delivery messengers
What they bring may not be what was asked exactly
But when the faithful examine,
It works perfectly,
Exceeding their imagination
No use complaining to the Lord
He knows our needs
He is God indeed

Many have asked,
Many have gotten
Many haven't appreciated
Many have forgotten
The Lord has forgiven
And He has given

It's there in front of the eyes,
If the eyes are open
The wise will realize,
Not leave a package forsaken

BANK

I'm saving in the bank for my future
I'm depositing all my treasure
Lord you're my bank
My soul is what I'm putting in
I know you pay great interest
You have my interest
My future is secure

Lord you're my bank
I know you'll never tank
My soul is safe with you
I give you it for safe-keeping
My soul is safe with you
My soul is saved with you

Lord you're my bank
My investment guarantees me life
The interest is eternal life
Everyone who did deposit has gotten it,
Except for who withdrew for failing of spirit

Lord you're my bank
Unto you I give thanks
I feel blessed with you there
I feel blessed enough to invest

Lord you're my bank
Any other bank is piggy bank
No one can convince me to switch

Lord you're my bank
Thanks for making the only fee morality

Lord you're my bank

HOUSE OF THE RISING SUN

Good souls sleep amongst angels
Rest well sweet darlings
The door of tomorrow cracks open,
Exposing the foyer of the morning
They walk in the tender light of the dawning,
Ready to occupy the day with confidence

Duty, tasks, masks, questions to ask,
News to come in the house of the rising sun;
Knowing who, who to know, what to know
Here comes the pain, the terrible insane,
Panting frantic in foot traffic, norm is panic
Sweet beauties flow along, calm in spirit

Angels always have a prayer in heart
They enter the day refreshed in spirit
Whatever comes they can handle it
Their mind whistles the Gospel
Their soul sings along
Their demeanor is ever calm

Saints hear the call of Heaven
They never cease praising
Their response is always Heavenly
They devour in the spirit of the Lord
Nothing around upsets their balance
They wear the crown of life in every instance

Sweet loves about to open the door to night
They leave the day behind with its harrowed plight
They enter darkness with Truth's light,

Having no guilt for the door they'll close
They performed in the wealth of conscience,
Ready to rest again in the presence of angels

THESE I ASK

Let my work be sanctified before the Lord
Lord give me courage to tread through the field of snakes
Let not the jaw of the fierce beast rip me apart
Protect me from the mighty dragon
Shield me in the land of Babylon
Remember me in your high place dear Lord
Receive my prayer with mercy
Let my faith never fail before your face
Turn not the air into a storm of dread
Pour showers of blessings from Zion instead
Brighten my face as Jesus transfigured
Let my shine be light unto men
Lift me up as your Son to Heaven
Lord let my days be numbered in righteousness
Write my story in the Book of Life as the tale of a saint
Treasure my picture on a wall in Heaven
Lord accord me the strength to accomplish what you wish
Endow me with wisdom as Solomon to know right from wrong
Enlist me in the ranks of warriors against evil
Lord for you I've worked so hard,
Let eternal life be my reward

LORD GOD HELP ME

I did what I could given what I had
Father, if you want more, give more
Surface in me the power of creation
Allot me might beyond imagination

In the rifted rock rolls a stream
In rough terrain it crafts a dream
To the glory of its end it meanders,
Its course a marvelous story to beholders

In my might let me carve a path
When the road is rocky, let me find a way
Let my twists and turns never drift my focus
Reward me with a history to an amazing locus

Imagine a world where sweat is the only truth you know
I have been drenched in the labor of your love
I demanded more of myself to bring out the best in myself
For your sake it seemed a pleasing thing

The spirit is willing, but the flesh is weak
Father, don't give up on me now
Strengthen me towards my vow
Render my talents worthy of my ambition

Lord show me the way when I'm blind to it
Wizen my mind so I resource myself properly
Give me time to finish this great work
Give me time to rest, rejuvenate, and reevaluate

Lord there's no failure in you
Unto you I give my whole soul
I'll live for you 'till I'm an old soul
I'll be ready for you when I'm only soul

I give my best to this time-space test
And ask that you take care of the rest
Make me blessed, make my work blessed
I pray you give me the power in my chest

BATTLING DEMONS

Battling demons in the world is a great fight for the righteous
Battling demons in your house makes your house contentious
Battling demons in yourself renders your life torturous

When the demons reside inside, you'll beg, "Lord cast out these demons. Throw them in swine, but remove them from my mind"
When demons are rooted so deep you lose sleep and always weep
Only constant prayer and firm faith can remove them
If you let up, they'll win
And you'll live in sin
They will control you,
Make you live a life that's not true,
A life impure and miserable
They'll make you not be you

When demons are about in your house,
All you want is to get out,
Or get them out
Cause they make you want to shout
You can't sleep at peace when they're about
For peace of mind they have to go
Or you must go

The world is full of them
They wreak havoc with their evil,
Causing the poor social conditions we're used to
And the bad politics and corrupt governments around
Demons destroy or manipulate the economy for themselves,
Never minding if their behavior harms anyone else
They're criminal minds making communities insecure
Righteous souls are ever in a fight against them
They're the ones in the fight for human rights,
And the great movements for independence
The fight against demons cannot stop
They won't stop, so any let up is a flop

RIGHTEOUS MOTIVATION

The world turns by the breath of God
As long as you have breath, you owe it to God
Be grateful rather than take it for granted
To the pleasure of the Lord, use it unabated

Don't fear anything; God has your back
Go do for Him and never think you lack
Whatever talent He gives, develop on His behalf
Use even a simple gift; Moses only had a staff

The Lord is willing to work through you,
If you're willing to let Him use you
Be captured by His Spirit,
You'll produce wonderful works of spirit

Let faith be your guide
And the Lord your pride
True love must motivate you
Hope must bring you through

You have beauty beyond measure
It surpasses words to capture
It's the loveliness of God
It resides inside and is accessible to you

Never let your body conceal your beauty
Find and expose it radiantly
It'll be a marvel for the world to see
It could change the course of history

Now you know the truth, you know your duty
Be true to yourself for your true self is your divinity
Don't bury your beauty for the sake of vanity
Reveal it for satisfying purpose and bettering humanity

RIGHT WITHIN

Hate clogs your heart
Anger eats out your soul
Love melts tension
Forgiveness eases distress

Where the mind wanders,
There the spirit goes
Where it rests,
There the spirit gets obsessed

The Lord writes within
It takes the third eye to see
And a clean heart to translate the writing
What's written is the right thing

Heaven is each man's core
Hell is any man's torture,
Driven by ego parting him from his nature,
Making him an enemy of nature

A strong mind can bend space and time
A resilient soul lives a victorious life
A healthy body makes for a healthy mind
Mind, body, and soul must properly align

Belly with the flesh of Christ will never hunger
Veins with the blood of Jesus exist in a body that'll never die
Tongue with the Word of the Messiah can never lie
Body fat with Him is trim for good living

Attend your ears to wisdom,
Lest your mind become numb with dumb
Do what's right in God's sight,
Lest you do what's wrong in your own

LORD YOU'LL BE THERE FOR ME

When my mother forsakes me,
When my father forsakes me,
When the world turns its back on me,
Lord you'll be there for me

When I can't seem to manage,
When I can't find a way out,
When I find myself in doubt,
Lord you'll be there for me

When love won't find me,
When solace is my company,
When there's no one to see,
Lord you'll be there for me

When the storm arrives,
When the Earth shakes,
When the flood inundates,
Lord you'll be there for me

When friends betray me,
When the crowd malign me,
When people deceive me,
Lord you'll be there for me

Lord I have no fear
You'll always be there
I can turn to you,
When I have no one else to turn to

Lord you're my comfort
You're my refuge from hurt
In you I find strength
I'll live by your love for life's length

GOD GETS ME

You may not get me,
But God gets me
And that's all that matters
To you, my life might be in tatters
I may not fit your scheme,
Might be failure in your dream
But I'm happy with the process,
As long as I'm making progress

Where you see trouble,
I see necessary struggle
You think I haven't hope,
But I can certainly cope
I'm not in with certain people,
But that's me maintaining principle
You might laugh or feel sad;
Not over me cause my life isn't bad

Go ahead and gossip,
It's God I worship
I don't watch any crowd
I stand loud and proud
I do things my way
And sleep well every day,
Cause I'm not doing wrong
And my spirit is ever strong

Go live your own life
Don't worry about my strife
I accept it for what it is
And mind my own business
You should do the same
And please leave my name
I'm living for God
And that's nothing odd

WON'T IDOLIZE PEOPLE

If you have a good word,
I'll listen
If you do a good work,
I'll follow
But I won't idealize you
I won't idolize you
You're not Jesus Christ,
Even though you're in Christ's seat
My expectation is of the Lord
And in Him is no disappointment

Man isn't perfect,
Though he's capable of perfection,
And should strive for it
But I won't think a man has achieved it,
Such that my faith is based on him
My faith is in God
I don't depend on middlemen,
Though I respect one preaching the Gospel,
Or even one appearing to set an example
I have my Bible
I can pray
I can meditate
I can seek to do better

It's not that I don't trust you;
I just don't put my trust in you
If you fail, that's on you
You won't break me too
But I'll pray for you
And ask that you be true

EVIL, WORLD OF EVIL

Oh my God! Oh my God! Oh my God!
This is a world of evil
Evil, evil, evil
Evil everywhere
Evil in all forms
Evil is the norm

Evil, evil, evil
There's no 'scaping,
No place to hide
Everywhere you reside

Evil, evil, evil
It's depressing to think
It's hard to sink in
That there's so much sin

Evil, evil, evil
Lord you're my hope
Loving you relaxes me
And sets me free

Evil, evil, evil
Lord your place is good
Reserve for me a space,
Too much evil in the human race

Evil, evil, evil
Lord help I pray you
Help this world of evil
Help people not to follow the Devil

LOVE LEADS ME ON

On the road of life I endure trials
The journey is rocky,
Beasts of all kinds attack
But love leads me on

When night falls, you're ready prey
Creatures of the dark heartily strike
In fear you might lose your heart
But love leads me on

The journey is long and weary
You may feel you don't have the energy
You may be exhausted mentally
But love leads me on

Sometimes you're in a maelstrom
Sometimes the storm may come
Sometimes the way may flood
But love leads me on

The skies could forecast threateningly
The Earth may shake beneath your feet
You could be oppressed by cold or heat
But love leads me on

Sometimes you have not what to eat
Some days you can't find a place to sleep
So many times you lose sweet sleep
But love leads me on

Sometimes you have company
Most times the journey is lonely
Disheartening when it's you only
But love leads me on

CROWD APPEAL

I will not be amused by evil men with their folly
My eyes won't be clouded by fame and glory
I won't cheer what's popular just for the sake of its popularity
Neither will I be beguiled by false charity

Satan draws many by cords of vanity
Many betray morality to be in a crowd
Many believers have fallen to hypocrisy
Too few value a true sense of identity

It's hard to be unique,
Especially when being special means being righteous
But it's better to be godly and by yourself
Than to be in company headed for Hell

POLITICS OF THE DAY

Regardless of who's in office,
God is in control
I'm not ignoring politics of the day
I just don't let it hold supreme sway
Politicians won't change my moral fabric
I won't put my trust in them
They can't take me to Heaven
They have a job to do
I'll do my best to hold them accountable
But I'll account for my life
And do my best to be my best

Politicians are men
And while we want the best of them,
Expect the best of them,
I won't be heartbroken by them
My hope is in the Lord

WHY SEEK JESUS

Believe on He from Galilee who walked upon the sea
He handles the sun, moon, stars, you and me
He died upon a cross to set men free
Only by His wisdom can men truly see

Those who were aggrieved
But who also believed
And Him they received
Were indeed relieved

Those who cried He heard,
Led them like a shepherd,
Made them preferred,
Freed them like an aerial bird

His touch is Heaven sent
Touch even the hem of His garment
It gives life as it's meant
The soul will find armament

In Him is the power,
Which moves creation every hour
To the soul, He's the tower,
Protecting it from need to cower

Of this world He's the light
To the soul He's delight
To the mind He's the right
To the victor He's the might

In His faith, one is healed
Through faith, He is revealed
By His faith, fate is sealed
With His faith, sin is repealed

HONEST WORD

Do men not give their word and break it?
By their word many men fake it
How can we trust men when time and again men have proven they
cannot be trusted?
The children, the animals bring us comfort
They're never deliberately evil
But man, man is a monster by his mind

As for us, we will trust in the Lord
The Word of the Lord is secure
Once spoken, it is never broken
And in it is life
We are comforted by it,
As it holds our promise

We will glorify the Lord
The Word of the Lord is the Lord
As our God is true,
So is His Word
We find salvation in it

LORD TOUCH ME

Lord touch me
I can't see
Lord touch me
I see men as trees
Touch me again Lord
I see men as devils
Thanks Lord
Now I can see
Thanks for showing me

If men could only see,
See themselves in reality
If men could only see,
They'd ask, "Lord save me
I'm really not free
I'm a slave within myself,
So I cry for help
Lord save me"

Men have become prisoners of their minds,
With souls lost in space and time,
Addicted to some devilish identity,
Living like vampires avoiding the light of Truth,
Living a lie by closing their third eye
But if Truth opened it,
They would cry, "Lord save me"

THE LORD HAS RISEN

The Lord stomps His feet in Zion,
The Earth shakes and quakes
When He stands from His holy seat,
The Mississippi rushes away like a snake
Saints in their camps sing praises
Angels raise the banner of Heaven
On Earth the Lord's beloved rejoice
All creatures submit to cheer or fear
The Lord God has risen
Hallelujah declares Heaven
The Lord God has risen
He has opened Heaven

Cherubims blow trumpets on the right and left
Standing to attention is Mount Everest
Sinners realize they have nothing left
The righteous sense peace and rest
Dumbfounded are leaders of nations
Astounded are all without premonition
The dead rise from their sleep
Gushing violently are fountains of the deep
The Lord God has risen
Hallelujah declares Heaven
The Lord God has risen
Hear ye, Heaven is open

In desperation sinners declare freedom from sin's slavery
Fallen to cowardice are those who once declared bravery
History turns a new page for the start of a new age
The Earth is thankful for relief from man's reproach
False pride cries in the face of true pride,
That exhibited by the humble and meek who did seek
Finding strength are those the world declared powerless,
While those who learn a lesson haven't another chance
The Lord God has risen

Hallelujah declares Heaven
The Lord God has risen
Hear ye, Heaven is open

SPREAD LOVE / WHO ARE WE?

Who are we in this fight?
We've said before and we'll say again
We go on behalf of the living God
We fight with love in our heart
We don't want to rip them apart
We just want to spread love
We want to spread love like a virus,
Have it infect the world like it infects us
The good shepherd infected us
Since then, it has affected us,
Made us conscious
And even ambitious
We want to spread this love inside us,
The Gospel of the Lord Jesus

Who are we?
We are those determined to save life
We are willing to sacrifice our life
Because Christ sacrificed His life
Success is saving at least one life
There's celebration in Heaven for each saved life
We go for the joy of Heaven in this life
Success is in giving all our life
We care not for any other life

Who are we?
We walk on higher ground,
Not of arrogance have we trodden,
But of the Lord God arisen
We're humble as lambs,
But with the pride of lions
We come as Christ,
Who died as a lamb,
But rose as a lion
We'll conquer as He does through the power of love

LORD HANDLE MY NEEDS

Give me the fruit of the land
And wisdom to understand
Give me the herb of the field
And knowledge to yield
Lord provide and reveal,
I'll be satisfied with the deal
As you turn the hands of time,
Cleanse my soul of grime
Father ever direct my mind,
So I always leave evil behind
Even to what I must be a novice,
Never let me fall to cowardice
Let the Earth be my palace
And you be my solace
When you blow the winds of change,
Let me never fear what may look strange
May my only hunger be for righteousness
And for that Lord, I ask you to bless
I only want a job of the living God
Father, I pray you give me the nod
In a world where there's much to worry about,
Lord let me never be swallowed by doubt
Lord God bless me, bless my family
Bless me as I dedicate this homily

GOOD NEWS

Radio, television, newspaper, online,
The news is always bad
It just makes you sad
Bad news, bad news, bad news,
Gives you the blues

Well, I've got good news,
The Gospel of Jesus Christ
Tell your friends and family
Spread it the world over
Who can hear, let him hear

Hear the good news
Jesus died to save us
He died for the remission of sins
Through His blood, we can be reborn
We can have everlasting life

Hear the good news
He died so all who believe shouldn't perish
He died and rose from the death
He's alive
Our God is alive

Hear the good news
On a cross He was crucified
On a cross He bore our sins
Take up your cross and follow Him
Your sins can be forgiven

Hear the good news
The Lord Jesus is our Savior
His love we can savor
Let's copy His behavior
With God we'll find favor

Hear the good news
Drink of His blood, eat of His flesh
You'll be refreshed
You can be reborn
And never know death

Hear the good news
Jesus promised us paradise,
If we live like His life
Our present troubles are no problem,
Compared to what we'll have in Heaven

Hear the good news
Jesus has a crown of life for us
He has a mansion in paradise for us
He sits on the throne of God
He is one with His Father

Hear the good news
Jesus Christ was the Messiah
He was a lamb to the slaughter
Now He's risen as the Lion of Judah
He's the King of kings and Lord of lords

Hear the good news
Jesus cares for us
He wants to save us
We must believe in Him
And forsake our sins

Hear the good news
Go spread it on the mountains
Go tell it in the valleys
Say it to the desperate
Remind believers, lest they forget

THE MESSIAH

At your birth, angels in Heaven rejoice
All creation is moved by your voice
The pure in heart make you their choice

On a mountain, the Gospel you preach
Your message goes beyond those you teach
Around the world, it's destined to reach

Who believes in you believes in your Father
It's you who good souls rather
In your spirit themselves they lather

You are the chosen of Heaven,
God's Son, the only begotten
By your mercy sins are forgotten

You're a friend that sticks closer than a brother
You love people more than their mother
You are to be chosen above any other

Heaven is your seat and the Earth your footstool
Wisdom is your domain and who rejects you is a fool
Proper for a man to submit to you as a tool

You are God on Earth
This is your right by birth
Who loves you knows not dearth

In you prophecies unfold
You're He who's spoken of in days of old
Only you fit the mold

You are Christ Jesus
Your life is miraculous
You're the Truth in all of us

DISCIPLES

Lord, we were only humble people
But you made us disciples
We had not much place on Earth
But you gave us place in your Kingdom

Lord, you esteemed us
And gave us a dream
You saw in us what the world didn't
You taught us as no one else could

Lord, how can we not love you?
You are our dream come true
You made us know God cares
Of your glory, you willingly shared

Lord, you gave us insight
And the faith to do right
You gave us triumph over devils
And the power to do miracles

Lord, we'll preach your Gospel,
As you authorized us to do
We witnessed to know you're true,
As your Father in Heaven witnessed you

Lord, you raised the dead to life
You did likewise to our spirit
In spirit and truth we worship
We live in your spirit for life

Lord, your faith gave us confidence
Your wisdom gave us moral sense
Your mission gave us purpose
We go to save life as you saved ours

TIME FOR PURPOSE

Fast as a cheetah,
Slow as a snail,
It doesn't matter,
Long as I get there

Why would I wake,
Except for Heaven's sake?
Lord if it's not for your purpose,
I may as well sleep to death

I'll do mine with my time,
You'll bless on your time
Lord just give me the sign,
And I'll follow the design

Some get it done quickly
They leave expeditiously
Others need to live longer
It doesn't really matter

Each man has his time
No one will go before
No one will go after
Success is what matters

Abraham lived 175 years
Jesus only had thirty-three
I'll take what's given me,
And give it all to God

I want to be fulfilled
I must live a fulfilling life
I'll have to fulfill my purpose
Doing so, I'll fulfill my time

STEP BY STEP

Lord, I'm mired in sin
I'd like to get out,
But I'm filled with doubt
I've made progress,
But I'm not there yet
Lord, help me step by step

Living in the dark, I know not light
I'm even afraid of the Light
But I know it's not right
I mustn't live this dark life
Lord, help me with my strife
Help me step by step

Lord, you walked amongst men
They saw you and found confidence
Immediately, they gave up their sin
But we must find faith in the unseen,
Have confidence in it to restore being
Help us make progress step by step

From Heaven, look down on us
But do not look down on us
Lord Jesus raise us up
Let us sup of your cup
Give us living water
Heal us step by step

Yes, I'll exert the effort
I'll look back and declare its worth
Perfection of faith will bring ultimate success
Optimism must eradicate pessimism
While I work on my faith and outlook,
Lord help me step by step

DON'T WORRY, BE HAPPY

Lord, just the mention of your name,
The thought of you brings peace
The pieces are just the same
But you'll fit them together

There's no need to be blue,
When you'll see things through
You see not as men do
But as what makes things true

It's good to try and try,
To never cease and say goodbye
But it's bad to think you're that guy
Who makes fate any which way apply

True, faith determines fate
But exactitude belongs to God
True faith expresses confidence
Humility shows good sense

Life is like a jigsaw puzzle
Man never sees the entire picture,
Only the pieces that confound
But the Lord sees where all fall

It's just a matter of time,
No need to worry the mind
He'll put the picture together
Its beauty will be displayed

Focus on the Lord thy God,
Not on confusion to drive you mad,
Not on futility to make you sad
God is in control and all will be fine

ADDICTED TO GOD

I'm addicted but I'm not sad
I'm addicted to God
Lord, I can't get enough of you
I love you,
Love praying to you,
Love reflecting on you,
Love reading about you,
Love discussing you

Lord, my whole life is about you
You're all I think about
I just want you in my system
My yearning for you is compelling

I can only keep company with who're into you
If they're not into you, I'll break away from family too
Lord, I'll die for you
Lord, I live for you

Because I'm addicted to you,
I can control myself with everything else
I lack self-control if I'm addicted to anything else
When I'm addicted to anything but you,
I hurt within,
I feel rotten in sin;
My soul feels corrupted

Lord, I want more of you
And when I get that,
I want more too
It's just where I'm at
You get me high
The high of you is incomparable
That's why I can't get enough of you

CATERPILLAR

Caterpillar on a leaf,
So humble, so meek
One day you'll fly,
Colored wings to dazzle the eye

Caterpillar I'm not jealous
The Lord made both of us
You have your destiny written
I'll have my metamorphosis too

Things are slow right now,
Not much happening really
But one day I'll fly,
With splendor to dazzle the eye

COMMUNICATION WITH GOD

You can never miscommunicate with God
He knows exactly what you mean
He hears not only your words,
He reads your mind,
Sees your heart

God knows all that's going on inside you
He knows your needs even before you ask
He's willing to take them to task
Asking shows respect;
It makes you humble,
And not take God for granted

SEASONS

When the winter is so cold
And the freeze has you in a hold,
Let the Lord warm you up

When spring lowers the cold
And springs its array of floral beauty,
Remember the Lord risen in glory

When summer dresses you with heat
And you feel you'll be up in smoke,
The Lord will prevent a heat stroke

When fall quails the leaves,
And leaves the ground with a pile,
Remember the Lord with a smile

When winter comes back blasting your back,
And the chill brings back the blues,
Let the Lord cheer you up

Be happy you're alive
And haven't taken a nose dive
You're witnessing God's hand at work

Your life to weather the weather,
Your body like the soul's feathers,
All God's great handiwork

Give God thanks in all things, great or small
Give God thanks in all seasons, cold or hot
Give God thanks in all times, good or bad

Give God thanks for provision
Give God thanks for life
Give God thanks for love in your life

DARING PROVERBS (DARINISMS)

Never entertain fools with their folly,
Neither partake in the entertainment of fools
Where there's prey, the predator follows;
Where there's sin, sinners gather
If you make yourself fake, you can't attract someone real
If you're real, fake people lose their appeal
Never be blinded by ego to sound decision
Never let indecision stifle your ego
The fool spends his youth in frivolity;
When he's old, he has nothing to show for it
A cup half-filled with good makes sweet drink
But a cup full of evil is as rum to the soul
Merry are the bands of men intent on wrong;
Sorrowful are they with the reward of damnation
Lift up your eyes to beauty in life
Let beauty dwell within your being
As a builder uses only what's necessary to construct,
Conserve your speech, lest you blabber like an idiot
As it's foolish not to walk when you have healthy legs,
Do not let your inner gifts wither away
You owe God everything,
But be thankful to helpful people

YOUR LOVE

You molded me from your love
Your love lifts me above
I've made up my mind,
I'll live for your love

I've made mistakes,
But I know what it takes
I've been off track,
But I've gotten back

Lord, I'm in your service
I know you'll bless plus tip
Nothing I wouldn't do for you
Your love makes me complete and true

No love could substitute for your love:
If I have all the love in the world,
But I don't have your love,
I would be miserable

If I had money in the millions,
All the comforts to be dreamed of,
The status of the most powerful man,
I wouldn't be satisfied without your love

Leave a space for my name in your Word
Call my name in your holy place
Reserve a space for me in your heart
You've occupied the entirety of mine

Your love forms the sinews of my heart
It pumps my heart to the tempo of Heaven
Your blood runs through it with every heartbeat
Lord, you're the fabric of my being

JESUS PAID

We sinned and should've paid the price
Jesus paid it all
His Father punished Him
To avoid punishing us
Jesus died for our sins,
Yet He was without sin
He was a victim
The lovely soul was a victim,
Murdered for our sins
He sacrificed and was willing,
So we wouldn't have to pay
He paid the price with His life
By His blood, we're redeemed
By His love, we're esteemed

God forgave us through Jesus
God gave up Jesus for us
God gave up His only Son,
A ransom for our sins
Jesus paid for us
Jesus prayed for us

Let us remember the blood that was shed
And how Jesus rose from the dead
His bloodshed saved us
His resurrection raised us
Let us praise Him
Let us love Him
He truly loves us

The Lamb of God took away the sins of the world
He paid in blood
We wouldn't have to face Noah's flood,
Wouldn't need to face Armageddon fire or God's ire
He gave His life to save us

Jesus paid for us
We owe Him
Let's pay with our souls
Let's pray, give Him control

Jesus saved us
Now, let us be saved
Through baptism in His blood,
Worship in His name,
And emulating His life

DON'T DESPAIR

When troubles hit you so bad,
If death is at your door, you'd gladly welcome him in
When your soul is so sad,
You just can't see a way to win

When you can't take any more,
Your head feels like it'll explode,
Your heart exposes a sore,
The burden feels like a heavy load

When you have no one to turn to,
Everyone seems just as miserable,
And you have to learn to
Bear the pain and be honorable

Don't despair my dear
Increase your faith and keep up the effort
Prayer does reduce fear
Continue in the Lord to deal with the hurt

Think about the Lord Jesus
In Him, put your trust
He'll take all the fuss
And bury it in the dust

Pray and believe in Him
You'll receive your blessing
Life won't be so grim
You'll see troubles lessening

With Jesus, life becomes pleasant;
You'll get the victory
Whether you're rich or a peasant,
Your story will be great history

WELCOME HOME

I got up this morning and saw God in front of me
The angels applauded
Of flesh I was free
The Lord said, "Welcome home, welcome home"

There was singing and cheer
There was merriment everywhere
I was lost and found
I'm home on Heaven's ground

I cried, for the life I knew died
But they were also tears of joy for the life I was about to enjoy
I prayed for loved ones left behind,
Wishing they'd likewise strengthen their mind

Oh what a merciless life it was,
Living in a world without love
It was rough sticking to the Lord
Now I'm happy I never went with the horde

Compared to eternal beauty, the temporary agony now seems minor,
Though in the life prior, the pain was major
But no need to dwell on a past destined to drift afar and drown in the ocean of time
My mind is set on timelessness, my maker and what He has to offer

The Lord God welcomed me in
To His home free from sin
I've been happy ever since
His words He didn't mince
He said, "Welcome home, welcome home"

BOSOM OF THE LORD

In the bosom of the Lord, I rest my head
My longing is arrested
My spirit is rested

In the bosom of the Lord, I rest my head
My heart is at ease
My soul is appeased

My fears evaporated
I'm feeling lifted
By grace I'm uplifted
I feel supremely gifted

He covers me with His arm,
Shields me from harm
His bosom is warm
His Word is a charm

In the bosom of the Lord, I rest my head
I'm raised from the dead
The Lord's bosom is my bed

In the bosom of the Lord, I rest my head
I'm calm as steady seas
Within, I'm truly pleased

My hope is justified
My soul is satisfied,
My truth verified,
My pride ratified

I can truly relax
Years of endurance was my tax
With God, I was never lax
My reward is His love to the max

SAVE MY LIFE PLEASE

Lord, save my life please,
Spare me this disease
I have people to live for
I have you to live for
I'm not getting any stronger
Doctors say not much longer
Lord, it doesn't have to be so
Please give me another go
Miracles are within your power
Grant me one this hour
Father, I have much to live for
As it is, I can have neither nor
Lord if this is for sins and lies,
I do apologize
My state is sorry, my fate is worse
Lord, only you can remove this curse
How much more fear must I swallow,
Knowing my future is hollow?
Lord, I beg you from the bottom of my heart,
For I'm here falling apart
I have so much more to give,
If only you would let me live
I'm not ready for the casket,
Or for my ashes kept in a basket
Lord, please hear my pleas
From this disease, give me ease
It's eating me out,
Limiting my ability to move about
On Earth, you touched and healed people
From Heaven, reach and restore me from this evil
Lord, Lord, Lord, make me adept as a player
Lord, Lord, Lord, take me, accept my prayer
Nevertheless, not as I will, but let thy will be done
I commend my soul to you as did your begotten Son

THE VOICE OF CONSCIENCE

In the halls of world leaders, the voice of conscience proclaims itself
Amongst kings and queens, it asserts itself
It is the King of kings and Lord of lords
Nations bow before it
It's the leader of a nation
From its station, it travels the world over
Mankind must listen to avoid war,
Render unto themselves its vision for true progress
Evil men try to kill it
But can men kill spirit?
The voice of conscience is the Head Creator, the Conquering Lion of
Judah, Earth's Rightful Ruler
There is no killing it,
The King is ever living

In the temples of men, the voice of conscience sounds,
Through priests and pastors to parishioners it redounds
From words on paper it emanates, percolates in air, seeps through ears,
awakes itself in the temple of primed minds
It prods with wisdom, prompts with Truth, uplifts with morality,
motivates with sanity
The wise allows it to conquer, knowing it always conquers, giving life
to those who obey, but rendering pain to the disobedient

The voice of conscience sustains the order of creation
In it is the vitality of all things,
For it is the King ever living
Creation listens to Him
Man must do likewise to avoid his demise

The voice of conscience eats time while it wrestles with the mind
It knows no borders, neither does it take orders
It orders all space, exists in every space, exists without space, exists
before space, exists after space
It's the saving grace of the human race

Its vision is unlimited and its power unrestricted
Wisdom is heeding its humble call in the mind
Wisdom is heeding its call through the man come to save mankind

CREST

Each moment is a crest in time where we could slide into the pain of a sordid past or slip into the hope of a bright future

Or we may ride the crest as a wave, stuck in the now, merely responding to the whims of time

Perhaps we may drown in the ocean of time, lost in memory as a nonentity

Or we may rise to the wave, control our footing, and sail into a glorious destiny

We may see the crest as a pinnacle for a panoramic view,

Assess whether we've done our best in the landscape of time

Maybe the crest represents our best and that's the level where we should rest

The crest could be a moment in isolation to hear the writs of our mind

Or it could mean that moment we assess those climbing towards us as friend or foe

Once we open our mind on the crest, we come to know

We can hear and see from the farthest reaches of time, appreciate what's left behind, and understand what's ahead

Maybe the crest is where we realize there are greater crests and we've got to keep climbing higher to see our clearest and claim our best

WE HOLD FIRM

Lord, you've struck your sword upon the land
How wretched are we of this generation:
The mother divided from the daughter; the father from the son
For your love, we've been rejected
For your love, we've not been dejected
We believe in your promise
And count this life as payment towards it
We pray for those foolish enough to sell themselves for the world
But we won't let their choice damn us

Lord, your Word resides in our hearts
It's all we live for
We love you first and foremost
For your love, we're willing to give up the ghost
We've ignored snares and stares
We've withstood derision
But we stand by our decision
Our bodies may be worn and haggard
Our countenance is hard,
But so is our spirit
We hold firm
For you, our spirit burns with desire
Better so, than have it burn in Hell's fire

INSPIRATION

Whoever you are,
Whatever you do,
Remember God loves you
Stay in the positive realms
Let no one remove your heavens
Everybody can't be your friend
You can't be everybody's friend
You know who you are?
You are special
What God expects of you is always better than what people expect
Always think you can do better than what others project
Compare yourself to the best person you can be;
Don't compare yourself to others
God gave you the life you live; you can handle it
Never take your life for granted; you aren't guaranteed the next minute
Push yourself to the limit and never regret it
But rest is valuable, so never forget it
Help where you can if you want meaning in your life
But don't try to give what you cannot, as that's foolish
Make faith a pillar of your life, as it's required for survival,
Much as good food is essential to a healthy body
You were made by grace, do everything with grace, lest you become a
disgrace

DISCOVERY

Behind the ugliness, there's incredible beauty
Within the madness, there's sanity
It takes patience; it takes calm
But it's there if you observe carefully

In the treachery, you'll find fortitude
From the loss, you'll find attitude
It's all about mindset
And the character you need to get

It'll all work out
Justice turns the hands of time
Good souls rise to the occasion
You just have to find your place in the scheme of it all

You'll overcome challenges that come
Within it all, you'll find wisdom
You'll understand yourself better
You'll become a better person

CALL ON THE LORD

I have mouth to speak,
So I'll speak
I'll call on the Lord,
Won't leave rocks to it
They'll be envious,
They won't get a chance
I'll claim my right,
It's just right

When I call on the Lord,
I'll do it with my all
Every cell will participate,
Likewise every space in between cells
Every tissue will,
Likewise every issue on my mind
Even hair and nails,
For no part of me must fail

I'll summon my pride,
Dedicate my dream,
My self-esteem unto the Lord
I'll take all my fears,
My length of years,
All my tears and give them to God

I won't hold back
When I call on the Lord,
Which I will continually as unrelenting duty,
I'll call with my all,
Words being symptomatic

Why should Jesus raise rocks to call on His name?
Should it only be amongst rocks that He claims fame?
Has He not already given us mouths?
Well, I'm going to shout it out,

Hosanna in the highest,
Blessed is He who comes in the name of the Lord
Christ's fame will be amongst every part of my being
And every part of my being will shout His name,
Won't give rocks a chance to do it

RIGHT RELATIONSHIP

This person is like me
That's why she likes me
And that's the way it must be
It's the work of God Almighty
If I choose, it would be calamity
I would select of my lust,
Go after my foolish imagination
But reality would come bust,
combust me in a stressful situation
Let God do His job
And "What God has put together,
Let no man tear asunder"

SPIRITUAL REVOLUTION

We need a revolution, spiritual revolution
The world is going the wrong direction
Mankind is drowning in sin
People are pregnant with hate and evil lusts
God has become an offense
People are casually immoral
They fear not consequence
Their behavior is getting worse
They're more desensitized to wrong,
Holding headstrong, claiming right as wrong and wrong as right,
And for such evil, demanding human right
Their society is breaking down spiritually,
Which means their society is breaking down;
Spirituality is the foundation of a strong society

The world needs leaders versed in scripture,
Individuals willing to buck the trend,
People willing to defend the Truth,
Those not concerned about ill-repute
The times beg the question, "Who will stand up for God?"
Should everyone fall abominably to lack of principle?
Should the situation disturb an ever receding few?
To be normal, people have to be radical
The good-hearted have to stand once and for all
They have to hold up the light of Truth in a dark world
Those enslaved by the power of conscience must act at its behest
This is what leadership requests
Without good guidance, doom is inevitable

The world situation is a test
The Devil is on the loose gaining power
He's getting more control over people's minds
They've been following him blind
It's time for the righteous to counter him on God's behalf
They must lead a righteous revolution

KNOWLEDGE OF SELF IMPORTANT

If you know not who you are, you'll be the dog trying to climb a tree
You can't have confidence without knowledge of self
That's like having a tree without roots

If you know not who you are, you'll be around negative people who drain your energy
If you have not knowledge of self, you won't have sound mental health

People crave happiness
Self-esteem is necessary for happiness
Self-love is necessary for self-esteem
You can't love yourself unless you know yourself
How can you love what you don't know?

You cannot love your fellowman unless you love yourself
You cannot love God unless you love yourself,
For in His image you were made
As to love yourself is to love God, and to love yourself is to know yourself,
You cannot love God unless you know yourself
You cannot love your fellowman unless you know yourself
(You cannot love God unless you love your fellowman)
(You cannot love your fellowman unless you love God)

You cannot find happiness without loving yourself
You cannot find happiness without loving God
You cannot find happiness without loving your fellowman
You cannot find happiness without knowledge of self

MAINTAIN HOPE

Regardless of how it looks, we must go into tomorrow with hope
There's better on the horizon
Now is just for a season
Let's use reason
And not do anything irrational
Let's calm ourselves,
Reflect on our options,
What we've done right,
What we've done wrong
We must remain strong,
Say a prayer and keep along
The victory will be ours,
As long as we persist
We must keep faith,
The Lord God exists
On Him we must wait
And know He will deliver,
For He's the Deliverer
For the good we do,
He'll see us through

YOUR CIRCUMSTANCE

It doesn't matter where you come from
Jesus came from a small city
It doesn't matter where you were born
Jesus was born in a manger
Don't let your circumstances hold you back
Poor mentality is worse than poverty
Strong minds make no excuse
Whatever is in the way, remove it
Whatever bad they say, disprove it
If there are obstacles, overcome them
Don't ignore problems, solve them

Look at what Jesus did
He changed the world
You can be just as big,
If you have faith and courage
Of course you need just cause
And the blessing of the Lord
Seek it in all you do
To God be true
To yourself be true
And keep pushing through
You'll make strides
You will rise
Keep your eyes on the prize

REGISTER

Sign up with the Lord,
The Lord is registering
He has a place of paradise
He is inviting you in
All you need is faith
And a life free from sin
The other fee is a good heart
And knowing your part

Register now, now is the time
One time, the Lord will shut the door
He hasn't told us when
Let's catch Heaven while it's open
Encourage others to do the same,
All are welcome in
But don't remain,
If they refuse to let go of sin

No man can save his brother's soul
It's better to enter half whole than stay whole in Hell's hole
Do the best you can, you're only human
Convince all you can to sign with God's plan
But don't let their recalcitrance put you in a trance:
Don't fall into their mindset or let it wither your faith
If of some people you must let go, do so
But don't make association with them a priority over Heaven

God's place is the place to be
There're angels, Jesus, and all free
There's only true love there
And not an ounce of fear
There's no sadness, no madness
There's just gladness and righteousness
Why are you waiting brother and sister?
There's nothing sinister, go register

DOOR OF CHRIST

Stand by the door of Christ
He's the way, the Truth, and the life
Enter in for better living

Stand by the door of Christ
It's the way to paradise
Enter into the glory of His Kingdom

There's no other way to Heaven
There's no side door, no back door
There's no window left open

You can't steal your way in,
Neither can you fake before Him
The only way is remission of sin

Stand by the door of Christ
It's the way to His reward
Enter into the joy of the Lord

Stand by the door of Christ
Gather there all ye saints
Enter and go marching in

Outside is just not nice
Inside is paradise
Go through Jesus Christ

The Kingdom of Heaven awaits
But don't wait
Let go ... and go to Christ

GOOD SHEPHERD

Come all ye sheep,
Follow the good shepherd
He'll lay down His life for you
He'll never flee when you're in trouble
He'll be there on the double

Come all ye sheep,
Follow the good shepherd
He is the Word
Gather in a herd
Obey His Word

Come all ye sheep,
Follow the good shepherd
He'll smite with the rod of correction
Take no offense and offer no defense
It's for your growth and protection

Come all ye sheep,
Follow the good shepherd
Ponder upon His Word
Wander not from the herd
Rest in His loving care

Come all ye sheep,
Follow the good shepherd
He's not the hireling who cares not
You are His flock
You're precious to Him

Come all ye sheep,
Follow the good shepherd
He'll guide you if you go astray
He won't forget you if you've lost your way
He'll celebrate on that day (you're found)

JOHN 11 VERSE 25

Jesus said, "I am the resurrection, and the life: he that believes in me, though he were dead, yet shall he live"

Do you want to live?
You can through Christ
The lust of flesh is death
The spirit of Christ is life
Be resurrected in His spirit
Be no more a slave of sin
Find your freedom in Jesus

Do you want to live?
Believe in Jesus, you shall
Faith in Him is life
He's the Savior of the world
You can be saved from the world
For this life is death
But the life of Christ is eternal

Do you want to live?
You shall live if willing
Recognize this world of sin
You can't have it and Christ's life
No man can serve two masters
Forsake lusts of this world
And you'll gain life in Christ
(John 12 verse 25: "He that loves his life shall lose it; and he that hates his life in this world shall keep it unto life eternal")

TEN PRIMARY STRATEGIES TO SPIRITUAL HEALTH

1. Love, the Lord thy God with all your might, with all your soul, and seek Him and Him only, and let Him be your reward.

2. Keep focused on Spirit with constant meditation and prayer.

3. Know and be yourself.

4. Remove yourself from evil influences, unless by your presence you're attempting to change them.

5. Relax, let God take charge and have faith that He will.

6. Treat every other human being as your other self, and as God's self in flesh, much as you must see yourself as God's manifestation.

7. Revere nature

8. Follow your conscience

9. Make your work God's work as your image must be God's image on earth.

10. Thank God for His blessings before asking for more.